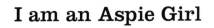

I am an Aspie Girl

of related interest

Parenting Girls on the Autism Spectrum
Overcoming the Challenges and Celebrating the Gifts
Eileen Riley-Hall
Foreword by Shana Nichols
ISBN 978 1 84905 893 3
eISBN 978 0 85700 612 7

Girls Growing Up on the Autism Spectrum
What Parents and Professionals Should Know
About the Pre-Teen and Teenage Years
Shana Nichols
With Gina Marie Moravcik and Samara Pulver Tetenbaum
ISBN 978 1 84310 855 9
eISBN 978 1 84642 885 2

My Autism Book
A Child's Guide to their Autism Spectrum Diagnosis
Glòria Durà-Vilà and Tamar Levi
ISBN 978 1 84905 438 6
eISBN 978 0 85700 868 8

I am an
Aspie Girl

A book for young girls with
autism spectrum conditions

Danuta Bulhak-Paterson

AFTERWORD BY Tony Attwood

Illustrated by Teresa Ferguson

Jessica Kingsley *Publishers*
London and Philadelphia

First published in 2015
by Jessica Kingsley Publishers
73 Collier Street
London N1 9BE, UK
and
400 Market Street, Suite 400
Philadelphia, PA 19106, USA

www.jkp.com

Library of Congress Cataloging in Publication Data
Bulhak-Paterson, Danuta.
  I am an Aspie Girl : a book for young girls with autism spectrum conditions / Danuta Bulhak-Paterson ; afterword by Tony Attwood ; illustrated by Teresa Ferguson.
      pages cm
  Summary: "Lizzie explains what it's like to have Asperger's Syndrome, including how she has a special talent for blending in with her friends, how she gets really tired after being at school all day, how she worries about making mistakes, and how she finds it hard to understand how she is feeling"-- Provided by publisher.
  ISBN 978-1-84905-634-2 (alk. paper)
  [1. Asperger's syndrome--Fiction. 2. Autism--Fiction.] I. Ferguson, Teresa, 1946- illustrator. II. Title.
  PZ7.1.B86Iam 2015
  [Fic]--dc23
                    2014039673

British Library Cataloguing in Publication Data
A CIP catalogue record for this book is available from the British Library

ISBN 978 1 84905 634 2
eISBN 978 1 78450 110 5

Printed and bound in China

My name is Lizzie and I love to draw. I live with my family and my dog and cat, Milo and Ollie. My favourite subjects at school are art and reading. I like my teacher at school and I have a nice group of friends.

In many ways I am just like my friends. We all like to laugh, play, and help each other. But there are also ways that I am different.

You see, I have Asperger's Syndrome. Asperger's Syndrome is now called Autism Spectrum Disorder, or ASD. People with Asperger's Syndrome have some real strengths. They are often smart, honest, kind and caring, and creative. They often have a special talent. This may be in art, science, music, reading, or computers.

But I am also more special because I am a *girl* with Asperger's Syndrome.

In fact, I like to say that I am an 'Aspie girl'. Girls with Asperger's Syndrome are often quite different from boys with Asperger's Syndrome. Keep reading and I will tell you why!

Aspie girls often have a special talent at being able to blend in with others and look just like the other girls.

It's like being an actress, I guess, where school is the stage.

But this is hard work and makes us tired! When I come home I really just need some time to myself.

Do you get really tired after being at school all day?

Our interests might be really similar to other girls' interests, like reading, art, technology, animals, or music, but we like to spend a lot more time on them. You know, it can be very hard to pull away from our interests. For example, I love Anime and can spend hours and hours drawing and then I don't have any time left to do important things like my homework or cleaning my room.

Some Aspie girls are not interested in 'girly' things at all.

Do you have an enjoyable interest that takes up a lot of your time?

What is your favourite way to relax?

Aspie girls can be really sensitive to feelings, which means we might feel really sad, scared, or angry really quickly and we don't always know why... You know, I often worry about making mistakes and think that I have to be perfect. This is scary for me! But my teacher reminds me that making mistakes helps me to learn.

Do you worry about making mistakes?

Sometimes I get really angry and scream and shout. This just seems to jump out of me and I don't mean to be like this. Afterwards I feel very sad.

What are some of your strong feelings?

We might get bothered by loud noises, strong smells and tastes, bright lights, or scratchy clothes when other people don't seem to notice these things. I don't like listening to some sounds because they hurt my ears.

Also, I have a very strong sense of smell and find some ordinary smells HORRIBLE!

Being bothered by such things is called having sensory sensitivities.

Are you bothered by some noises, smells, lights, tastes, or feelings on your skin?

Aspie girls are friendly and want to have friends, but it can be tricky for us to know how to play together happily.

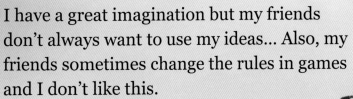

I have a great imagination but my friends don't always want to use my ideas... Also, my friends sometimes change the rules in games and I don't like this.

This means that I sometimes have no one to play with and end up feeling like I am an outsider. It's a shame because I have a lot of fun ideas.

Aspie girls can find it hard to share their feelings with people. It is hard for me to tell my friend if I feel happy, sad, or grumpy. Sometimes I don't even know how I'm feeling.

Many Aspie girls find it easy to share their feelings with animals. I love my dog so much and he always knows how I feel!

Do you sometimes find it hard to understand how you are feeling?

Do you have a special furry friend?

Aspie girls can find it tricky to read people's faces. This has nothing to do with reading books – that is easy! Trying to guess how people are thinking or feeling by looking at their faces is *hard* work.

Here I am with my teacher and I can't tell if she is happy or angry with me.

Do you sometimes find it tricky to read people's faces?

Aspie girls may find playing
in a group hard and they
may have one special friend
who they like best.

When my best friend is not at school I feel lost and
don't know what to do. When she is at school I
find it really tricky to share her with other people.
Sometimes she likes to invite other kids to play
with us and this is tough for me.

Do you find playing in a group tricky?

Do you find it hard to share your friend?

But I am a good friend and when my friend needs me I am the first one there to help her out. I'm also loyal and stick up for my friend when others tease her.

Aspie girls can get upset when new things happen or when plans change. When this happens to me it feels like my whole world has been tipped upside down.

Moving house was really hard for me, even though it was only two houses away.

Do you get bothered or upset by changes or when things don't happen the way that you expect?

SOLD

One-page story

Being an Aspie girl means that although my brain thinks differently to other people it is still a smart and imaginative brain.

My teacher tells me that I have a great future ahead of me, with many wonderful talents to show the world!

Afterword

Sometimes the best books are the shortest books. This book does not have many pages but the text is succinct and clearly and accurately describes the characteristics and experiences of girls who have an autism spectrum condition (ASC). Each illustration is worth a thousand words and will be perceived as engaging and enjoyable for young children, adolescents, and adults.

I recommend this short and insightful book to parents, teachers and colleagues as an easy-to-read explanation of ASC in girls, and to the girls themselves to explain their everyday thoughts, emotions, and experiences to those who need to know.

While we have many books on boys who have an ASC such as Asperger's Syndrome, we have very few books specifically written for girls. Danuta's descriptions will contribute to a greater understanding of why the girl who has an ASC is different, and the girl herself will have greater insight into how her differences can become qualities.

Each copy of this book will probably be read and enjoyed by many people, and I suspect read frequently by the girl for whom the book was bought. Please ensure that those who borrow this book return the book for others to benefit from the insights and wisdom.

Tony Attwood
Minds & Hearts Clinic, Brisbane, Australia

For Parents and Professionals

It is becoming more understood that girls on the autism spectrum, who have a diagnosis of Autism Spectrum Disorder (ASD), Asperger's Syndrome, High-Functioning Autism, or Pervasive Developmental Disorder Not Otherwise Specified (PDD-NOS), present quite differently to boys on the spectrum. Some of the more obvious differences have been identified in this book. Generally, high-functioning girls on the spectrum present more subtly compared to boys on the spectrum. They can be natural mimics, often observing their peers and copying what they see. They can be shy, polite, and passive in their play with their peers. They may have a best friend. Their interests may not be unusual at all in topic, yet they may display an enduring intensity that may only be evident in the safety of home. Indeed, they may have some great strengths and may be talented artistically or self-taught readers. Ironically, although adaptive, their ability to mask their difficulties and mimic can lead to high levels of anxiety, self-doubt, and a poor self-image, where they may not know who they actually are themselves.

Unfortunately, most girls on the spectrum experience high levels of anxiety. This anxiety may be seen in their extreme perfectionism, and fear of making a mistake, trying new things and being themselves. Sadly, all these characteristics may lead these girls to being missed diagnostically, falling through the cracks, or often being misdiagnosed. For example, those with obvious anxiety may receive an anxiety disorder diagnosis and, though treatment may lead to some improvement in their levels of anxiety, they will continue to struggle at school and at work. Many women who receive an ASD diagnosis later on in life report feeling a great sense of relief upon receiving their diagnosis and believe that, had they received it earlier on in life, much confusion and difficulty with coping in life could have been spared. They may have been misdiagnosed with Borderline Personality Disorder or Bipolar Disorder and felt that this diagnosis did not quite fit or explain all of their difficulties.

As parents and professionals wishing to support girls on the spectrum, I feel that it is important not only to have a thorough understanding of autism spectrum conditions but also to adopt a positive attitude about the conditions. Genuine appreciation of the wonderful gifts that come with a different way of thinking will be infectious and will go so far in helping our girls value themselves and their different way of thinking. So many girls on the spectrum become women who doubt their self-worth, experience negativity in their social interactions, and feel misunderstood by others. We as parents and professionals can do so much to prevent and reverse this cycle by genuinely celebrating this different way of thinking and being accepting of and knowledgeable about it. ASD is not an illness and people do not 'suffer' from the condition. In fact, we are fortunate to have advanced in our society thanks to so many talented people with ASD sharing their skills in technology, science, medicine, and humanities.

A positive and celebratory attitude comes from knowledge and awareness. Becoming more knowledgeable about ASD will involve reading, attending seminars and lectures, and consulting with professionals who specialise in autism spectrum conditions to discover the strengths of this unique way of thinking. This positive appreciation of ASD can be communicated to your daughter through statements such as:

'You have a wonderful, healthy, and clever brain that works differently.'

'You think differently and that is great!'

'You are unique and we love you for that reason.'

'You are so interesting and I love that about you.'

All children deserve to be celebrated, cherished, and supported to be able to achieve to their fullest potential. Maintaining a positive and knowledgeable approach to ASD will certainly help our girls with ASD to do so.

Why I wrote this book

In my practice as a Clinical Psychologist, I found there was a great need for a resource to give to girls after receiving a diagnosis of an autism spectrum condition. A resource that they, as girls, could relate to, which recognised and celebrated the female presentation of Asperger's Syndrome or ASD. Although many books were available to help children develop self-awareness about their diagnosis of ASD, I found that these resources were typically skewed to the better-known male presentation of ASD. Being a unique cohort, many girls on the spectrum simply did not identify with the books that were available. Also, due to the lack of public (and even professional) awareness of the female presentation of ASD, the few examples of peers that the girls had come across with the diagnosis were boys, who presented more obviously and to whom the girls did not relate. And so I wrote this book.

I have written this book so that it can be read by, and to, girls who are trying to understand their diagnosis of Asperger's Syndrome or ASD. Some pages have questions at the bottom, which can aid further discussion and will make the book more specific and tailored to each reader. I suggest that a familiar adult gently explores the discussion points from the next section with a girl with ASD when she is experiencing these differences, to help her understand why.

Discussion points to explore with the child

The following discussion points are ideas for how this book can be used to maximise a girl's self-understanding and acceptance of a diagnosis of Asperger's Syndrome or ASD. They are categorised by theme, with the page number of the relevant section of the story written in brackets.

Exhaustion (page 5)

The ability to observe and mimic others can take an emotional toll on girls with ASD. They will arrive home from school emotionally exhausted from a day toiled with interpreting social demands and containing the associated high anxiety levels. After school it is common for girls with ASD to need time to de-stress and unwind in the safe haven of home. They may not have much to say when you ask them about their day. Do not push them for information. In addition, homework demands may be met with a high degree of reluctance and may create a source of conflict.

When exploring this point with a girl:

- Discuss her demeanor upon returning home from school. Help her to become aware of any fatigue and/or desire to spend some time alone.

- Ensure that you are understanding and supportive of her desire for solitude after school.

- Determine whether the pressure of homework is adding to her exhaustion and, if so, plan to meet with her teacher to discuss appropriate arrangements.

Special interests (page 6)

For girls with ASD, it is not necessarily the *topic* of their special interest that is odd (for example, drainpipes, levers, or a specific type of vehicle) but, rather, it is the *intensity* of the interest. Girls are often interested in typical peer-related topics such as arts and crafts, animals, music, television shows, and pop stars. Science fiction and fantasy are also popular genres for some girls. Whereas some girls may not have a long-lasting special interest, they may have periods of intense pursuit of a particular topic or task.

When exploring this point with a girl:

- Focus on the *intensity* of the interest. Perhaps she likes to spend a lot of time drawing or colouring, watching *Dr Who*, or researching tigers, for example. Help her identify this interest and explore how she finds it so very hard to stop this activity and move on to something else.

- Do not make her special interest a negative. Celebrate that it is a very important thing for her to do, which helps her to stay calm and develop intellectually.

Perfectionism (page 7)

Fear of making errors and a sound appreciation of order drives perfectionism in girls with ASD. Perfectionism in girls can manifest in their reluctance to try something new or go first in an activity, and difficulty coping with making mistakes. For example, some girls will screw up their drawing and start again if they make an error.

When exploring this point with a girl:

- Explain that mistakes are OK! Help her to understand that mistakes are part of life and everyone makes them. Parents, teachers, scientists, and artists *all* make mistakes, and that is normal.

- Explain that mistakes help us to learn. When students make mistakes at school or in homework, it helps teachers know what to teach their students to help them become smarter. Making a mistake in your artwork, for example, can help you overcome a challenge and build your artistic skill through practice and repetition. Making a mistake that upsets your friend is OK as long as you can apologise.

- Help her learn how to cope with making mistakes by reacting to your own mistakes in a calm and rational manner. Point out your own mistakes and show that you are OK with them.

Poor emotional awareness and management (pages 8 and 13)

Girls with ASD can experience very high levels of anxiety, sadness, and anger. However, they may have limited insight into their feelings. They may have a general sense that they feel bad but not know why. They may not know that it's possible to feel better, and may therefore feel apathetic about trying to deal with their feelings. Emotions may be released as a rage meltdown or a withdrawal meltdown. Many girls with ASD can contain their discomfort at school but upon reaching home can no longer hold it in, and so this is where it is released. An innocuous request from a parent may be enough to trigger their rage. Alternatively, she may come home and lock herself in her bedroom, refusing to spend time with family, perhaps preferring the company of a family pet. Girls with ASD may be extremely sensitive to the emotional atmosphere in an environment and a negative or tense environment may trigger a meltdown. They may sense that something around them feels 'not quite right' but be unable to label the feeling either in themselves or in others. However, a strong and overwhelming sense of empathy towards animals may be obvious.

Due to these issues in understanding and managing emotions it is important for girls with ASD to work with a psychologist on affective education and emotion management to develop skills to manage their emotions.

When exploring this point with a girl:

- Discuss specific times when she has lost her cool and explain that you know she was not being naughty or bad but that it was genuinely a really hard time for her.

- Help her realise that this is part of being an 'Aspie girl', or having Asperger's Syndrome or ASD. Say that you want to help her feel better during these times and that you are also learning how to do this.

- Validate the difficulties she has identifying and sharing her emotions. For example, you might say, 'You are so good at talking about [*insert special interest*], but sometimes it is hard for you to talk about your feelings.'

- Does she have a natural affinity with animals? Explore whether spending time with the family pet helps her to feel calm.

Sensory sensitivities (pages 9 and 10)

Girls with ASD often have hyper- or hyposensitivities to their sensory environment. Hypersensitivities to sensory input can be seen in attempts to avoid certain sensory input due to feeling overwhelmed by exposure to it. For example, putting their hands over their ears to block out sound, complaining about a smell, withdrawing from being touched. On the other hand, people with hyposensitivities to sensory input are undersensitive to certain stimuli and may have trouble processing the sensation of it, which can manifest in an attempt to seek out more of that sensation. For example, repeatedly smelling something, continually rubbing their hand over an item, wanting very strong hugs.

When exploring this point with a girl:

- Help her to identify her hyper- or hyposensitivities. She will really need your help here. Does she find some sounds painful to listen to, or does she seek out certain sounds? Is she fussy with food, avoiding certain flavours and textures, or does she seek out spicy and strong flavours? Does she complain of smells often, or does she frequently smell objects around her? Is she jumpy with physical contact, avoiding hugs, or does she actively rub her hands on items? Help her to identify examples specific to her and explain that these are called sensory sensitivities.

- Help her to see that some sensory sensitivities may be really helpful for self-soothing. For example, going to sleep with her soft, familiar 'blanky' makes her feel nice and calm. To manage distressing sensory sensitivities, remind her that you will be helping her understand and cope with these. Working with an occupational therapist who specialises in ASD will also be a valuable support to help minimise her distress and discomfort.

Reading people's expressions (page 14)

Despite having an ability to perceive the emotional atmosphere in an environment, girls with ASD may struggle to accurately read emotion in people's faces. For example, they may miss the subtle changes in their teacher's face in the classroom that indicate he is getting frustrated with a student and then receive a great shock when he becomes angry. They may not detect the disappointment in their friend's face when she finds out she was not selected for a part in the school play and continue playing as if nothing happened. As a consequence they may come across as insensitive, though this is not the case. At other times they may notice a change in facial expression but be confused by it and unable to identify which emotion it is.

When exploring this point with a girl:

- Ask her if she sometimes wonders what people might be thinking or feeling. Use a recent example and validate her confusion. For example, you might say, 'You are so smart at reading books, but reading people's faces is a lot harder, isn't it?'

- Encourage her to practise asking for assistance if she is having difficulty reading a face. For example, she could ask the person how they are feeling if she cannot guess. She could say, 'Are you OK?' or 'What can I do to help?'

Social confusion (page 15 and 16)

Girls with ASD may not stand out at first glance. Their ability to blend in and camouflage social confusion through observation and mimicry is a skill that masks their challenges. Unfortunately, this creates stress and exhaustion and contributes to them experiencing meltdowns upon returning home from school. Some girls also have an intense reliance on another peer at school. This peer is usually someone who has been kind and nurturing to them and they may refuse to go to school if they know this person will not be there. Once at school they may not want to share their friend and their anxiety will increase if their friend wants to play with other peers. For older girls this peer may be someone from an undesirable clique and the girl on the spectrum may be vulnerable to predators. For this reason, friendship groups should be monitored.

When exploring this point with a girl:

- Help her to identify a special friend she might have and what sorts of things they like doing together. Does she prefer to play with that friend alone?

- Explore whether she finds it difficult to share her friend. Validate her feelings about this and explain that true friends are like rubber bands and will bounce back if she lets go a little. If her friend likes to play in a group ensure she gets enough one-on-one time with her special friend outside of school.

- Help her to identify her positive social qualities. For example, she may be very kind, generous, loyal, and have a strong sense of justice. Praise these qualities when you see them in action.

Change (page 17)

Coping with change is often a great challenge for girls with ASD. Change can encompass a wide range of factors – from bigger life events, such as moving house, to the seemingly minor activities of life, such as transitioning from one activity to another. The degree of difficulty coping with various changes will vary from girl to girl. Some girls are more greatly affected by minor changes – for example, if furniture is moved in the house – but will seem to cope quite well with a more significant change like moving house. Other girls seem to be quite flexible with day-to-day transitions but react to bigger changes as though their world has ended. Understanding the importance of predictability and familiarity for girls with ASD and trying to accommodate this will go a long way in settling their anxiety.

When exploring this point with a girl:

- Discuss her preference for order and predictability. Use examples that are familiar to her and observed on a daily basis. You might say, 'I've noticed that you always like to eat your breakfast before you get dressed in the morning. You don't like it when I ask you to get dressed first,' 'Do you need to know what's happening next at school?' or 'What about at home? Do you like it when we have to go out suddenly?'

- Help her to correlate her upset mood and associated behaviour with changes that have occurred. For example, you might say, 'Remember the other day when we decided to go out for dinner and you got really upset and refused to get changed? Well, I think the reason for that may have been that we didn't give you enough notice that we were going out for dinner. You were already settled at home for the night. Do you think that could be possible?'

Danuta Bulhak-Paterson is a Clinical Psychologist and Director of Unique U Psychology, a psychology private practice specialising in females with autism spectrum conditions in Melbourne, Australia.

Teresa Ferguson retired from journalism to enjoy writing and video-making. Drawing and painting is her old hobby. When she 'met' Lizzie, the temptation to pick up her crayons was irresistible because, being an Aspie herself, she immediately identified with the character.